Great and Precious Promises

BIBLE VERSES AND CHILDREN

photographs by Jana Taylor

Great and Precious Promises

BIBLE VERSES AND CHILDREN

concept and photographs by Jana Taylor

The Christian Science Publishing Society

Boston, Massachusetts U.S.A.

For their loving support of my work I would like to thank: Beverly DeWindt; Brian Clendenen; the members of Twentieth Church of Christ, Scientist, Venice, California; Norm Bleichman; Michael Hamilburg; Allen Stump; Helen Bishop; Nancy Stimac; Kelly McDermott; Lori Kelly; Harriet Posner; Nancy Lindemeyer; Marie-Lucie Charlot; *Victoria* magazine; and especially my precious grandmother, Mary Chernsky. Thank you to Louis M. Perretta for giving me my first camera. Thank you to The Christian Science Publishing Society. Most importantly, I would like to thank our Father-Mother God, who makes all things possible. — J.T.

Publisher's Cataloging-in-Publication
(Provided by Quality Books, Inc.)

Taylor, Jana
    Great and precious promises : Bible verses and children /
concept and photographs by Jana Taylor. – 1st ed.
    p. cm.
    Preassigned LCCN: 97-76739
    ISBN: 0-87510-336-7

    1. Bible—Quotations—Pictorial works. 2. Children—Pictorial
works. 3. God—Promises—Pictorial works. I. Title

BS618.T39 1997   242'.5'022
                                      QBI97-41313

This book is dedicated to my son and friend
Michael Taylor Perretta,
who because of his beautiful inner being
made me aware of the magnificence of all children.

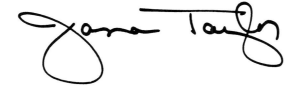

...his divine power hath given unto us all things that pertain unto life and godliness, through the knowledge of him that hath called us to glory and virtue: Whereby are given unto us exceeding great and precious promises...

The Bible, II Peter
King James Version

Foreword

Perhaps the dearest promise of the Bible is that each person's truest self is the child of God. The prophet Hosea wrote, "it shall come to pass, that in the place where it was said unto them, Ye are not my people, there it shall be said unto them, Ye are the sons of the living God." Malachi asks, "Have we not all one father?" And Paul writes, "I will receive you, and will be a Father unto you, and ye shall be my sons and daughters, saith the Lord Almighty."

Bible verses and pictures of children fit together so naturally.

For those reaching out to God, the inspired Word of the Bible has always offered truth and comfort, hope and salvation.

In a similar way, children have always embodied the promise of a better future for humanity—the promise of peace, the promise of grace and innocence and love.

In the infinite variety of children, there is yet a remarkable kinship, an undeniable common ground of goodness and purity. It is to the children of all ages and all nations that the Bible's great and precious promises are made, and kept.

And God saw every thing that he had made, and, behold, it was very good.

Genesis 1:31

As for me, I will behold thy face in righteousness:
I shall be satisfied, when I awake, with thy likeness.

$\mathcal{P}$salms 17:15

I will praise thee, O Lord, with my whole heart;
I will shew forth all thy marvelous works.

*P*salms 9:1

Thou openest thine hand,
and satisfiest the desire of every living thing.

Psalms 145:16

I will take you one of a city, and two of a family,
and I will bring you to Zion:
And I will give you pastors according to mine heart,
which shall feed you with knowledge and understanding.

Jeremiah 3:14, 15

Behold, I send an Angel before thee,
to keep thee in the way,
and to bring thee into the place
which I have prepared.

Exodus 23:20

The Lord bless thee, and keep thee:
The Lord make his face shine upon thee,
and be gracious unto thee.

Numbers 6:24, 25

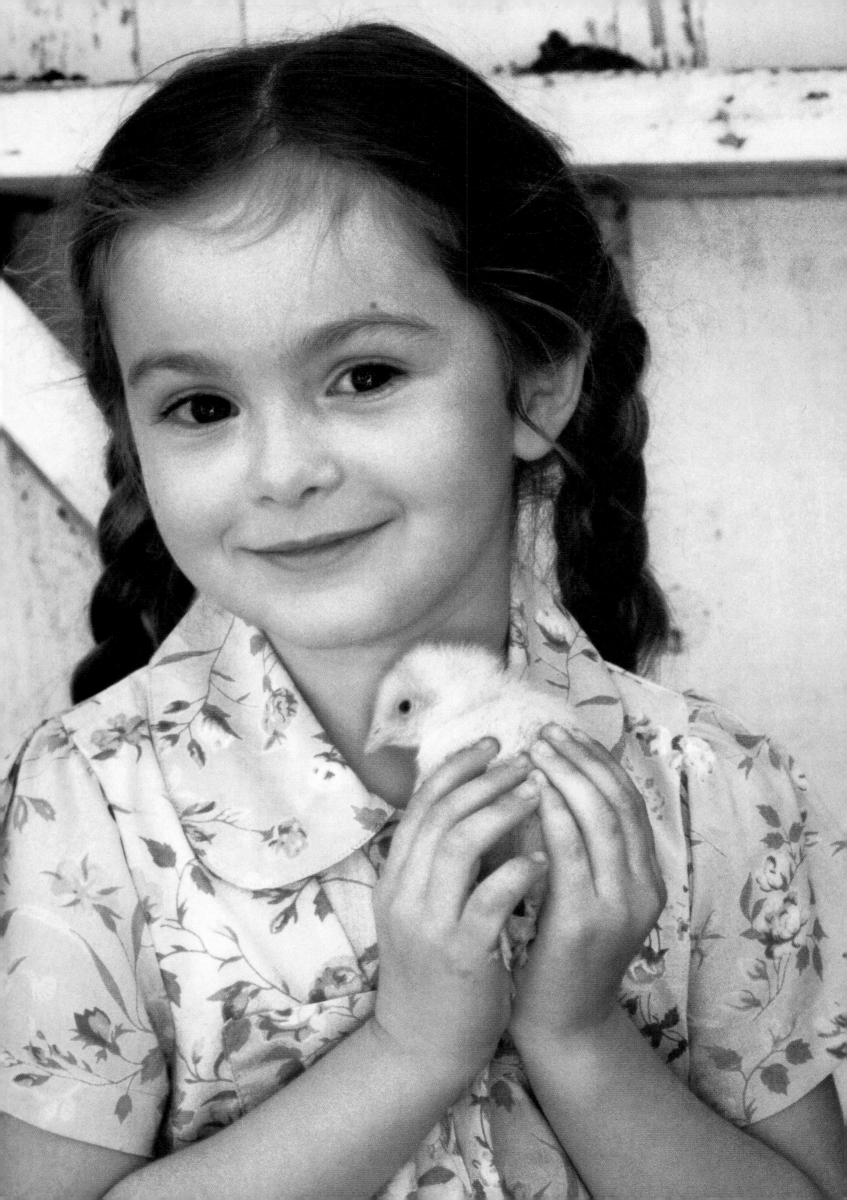

He performeth the thing
that is appointed for me:
and many such things are with him.

$\mathcal{J}$ob 23:14

We all, with open face beholding as in a glass the glory of the Lord,
are changed into the same image from glory to glory,
even as by the Spirit of the Lord.

II Corinthians 3:18

If I take the wings of the morning,
and dwell in the uttermost parts of the sea;
Even there shall thy hand lead me,
and thy right hand shall hold me.

$\mathcal{P}$salms 139:9,10

God is not the author of confusion, but of peace.

I Corinthians 14:33

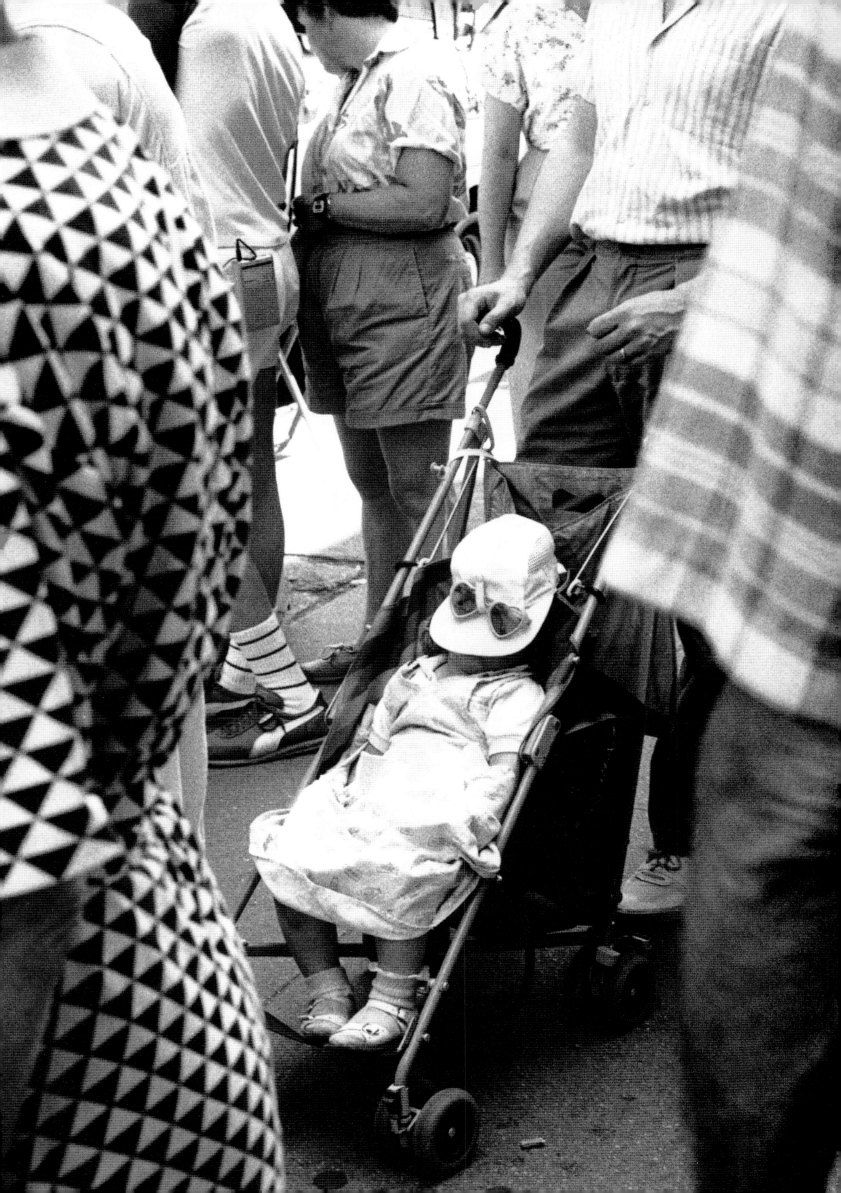

Delight thyself also in the Lord;
and he shall give thee the desires of thine heart.

Psalms 37:4

Arise, lift up the lad, and hold him in thine hand; for I will make him a great nation.

Genesis 21:18

Thou art ever with me, and all that I have is thine.

Luke 15:31

Whatsoever things are lovely,
whatsoever things are of good report;
if there be any virtue,
and if there be any praise,
think on these things.

$\mathcal{P}$hilippians 4:8

God is able to make all grace abound toward you;
that ye, always having all sufficiency in all things,
may abound to every good work.

II *Corinthians* 9:8

Their soul shall be as a watered garden; and they shall not sorrow any more at all.

Jeremiah 31:12

When he giveth quietness,
who then can make trouble?

*J*ob 34:29

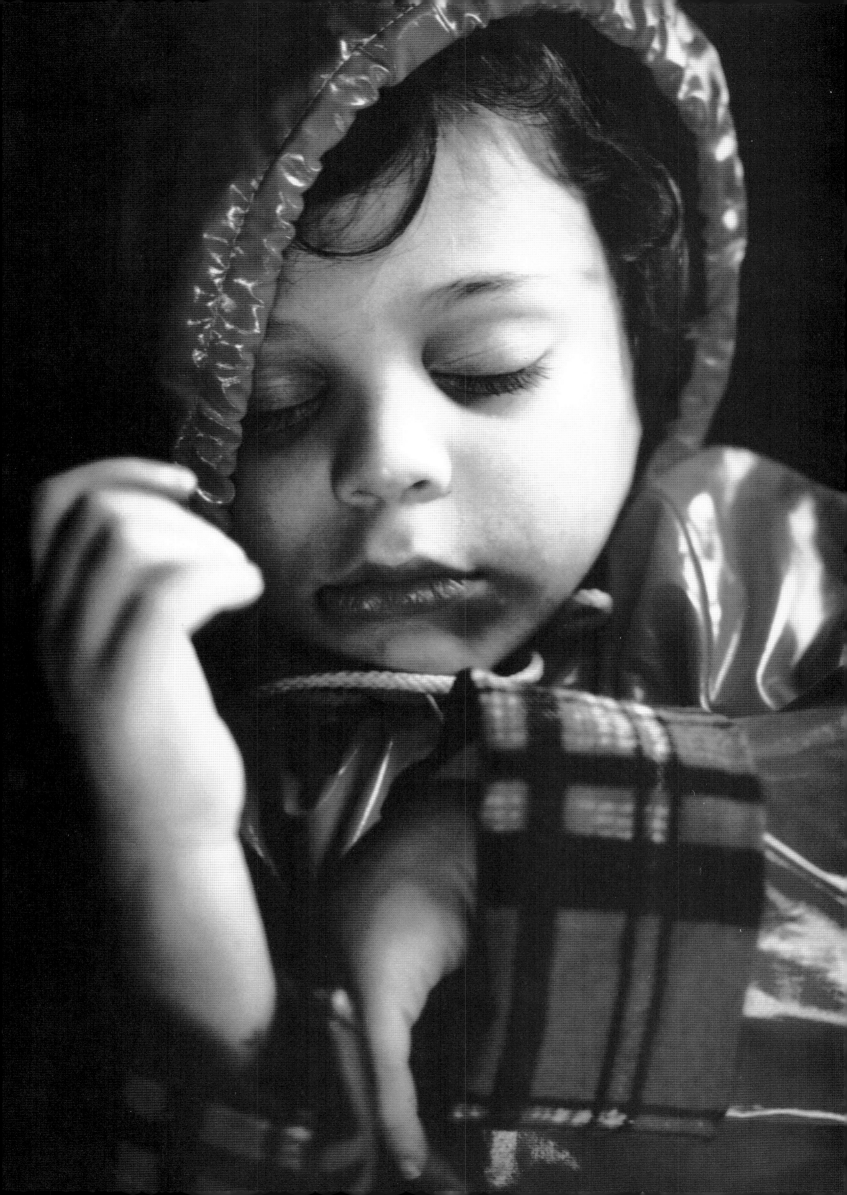

Every good gift and every perfect gift is from above,
and cometh down from the Father of lights,
with whom is no variableness,
neither shadow of turning.

James 1:17

Ye shall seek me, and find me,
when ye shall search for me
with all your heart.

Jeremiah 29:13

The Lord shall preserve thy going out
and thy coming in from this time forth,
and even for evermore.

$\mathcal{P}$salms 121:8

Blessed are the pure in heart: for they shall see God.

Matthew 5:8

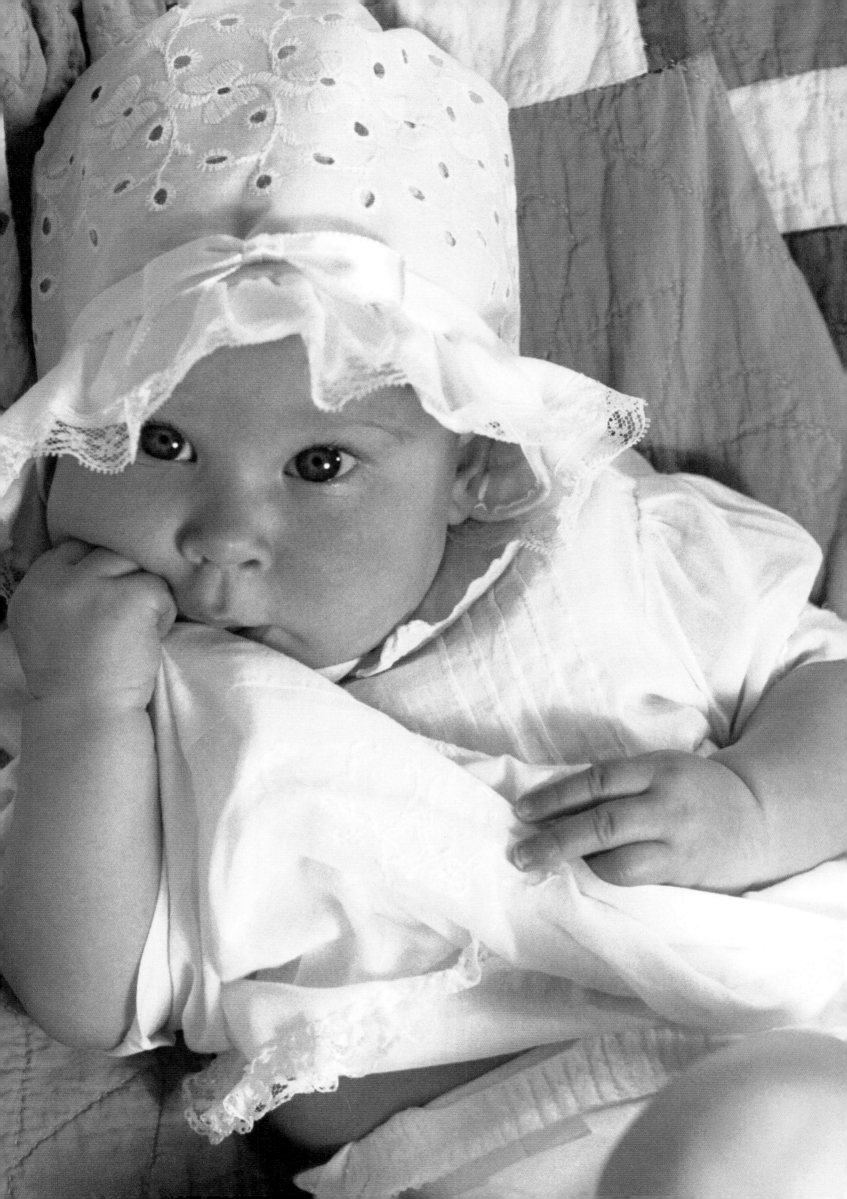

Lord, thou hast been our dwelling place in all generations.

$\mathcal{P}$salms 90:1

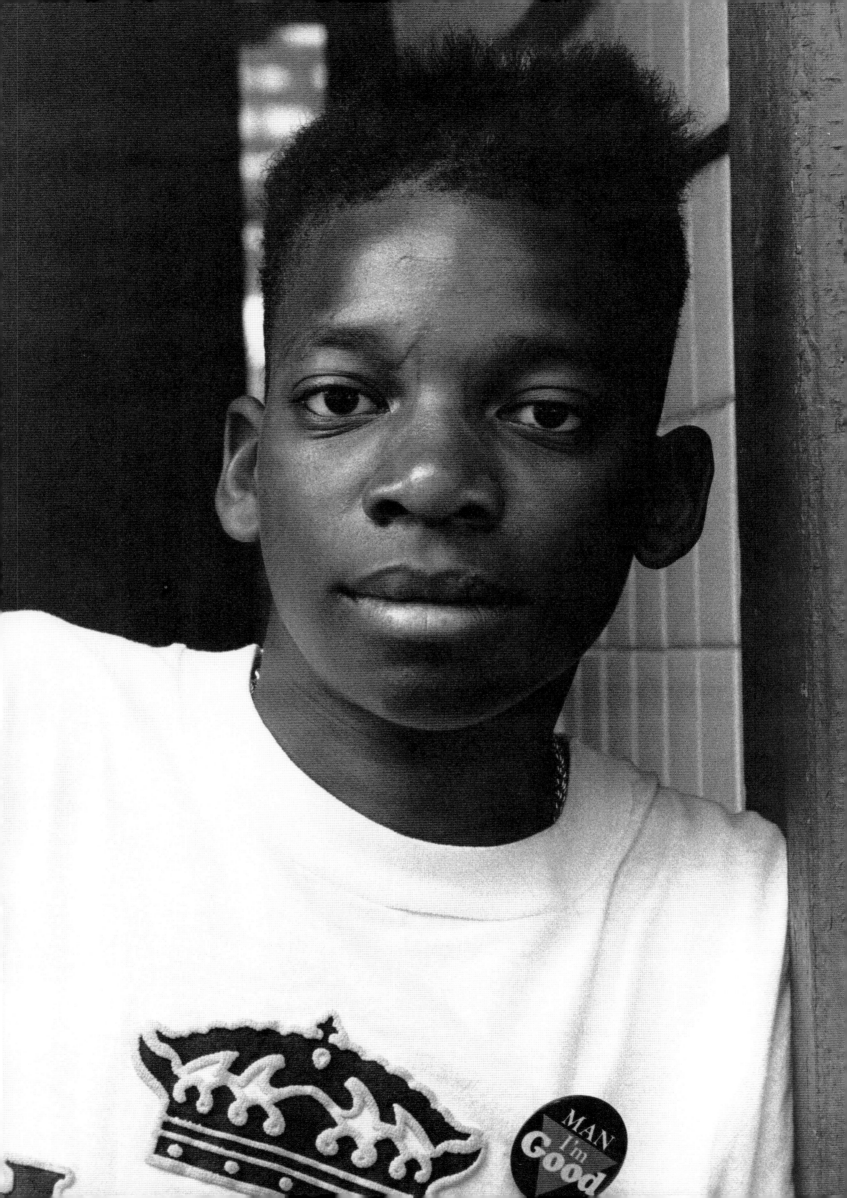

God giveth to a man that is good in his sight
wisdom, and knowledge, and joy.

Ecclesiastes 2:26

Thy right hand hath holden me up,
and thy gentleness hath made me great.

*P*salms 18:35

They that wait upon the Lord shall renew their strength;
they shall mount up with wings as eagles;
they shall run, and not be weary; and they shall walk, and not faint.

*I*saiah 40:31

The Lord shall open unto thee his good treasure.

Deuteronomy 28:12

Ye are the light of the world.
A city that is set on an hill cannot be hid.

Matthew 5:14

The Lord will give grace and glory:
no good thing will he withhold from them
that walk uprightly.

Psalms 84:11

The meek will he guide in judgment:
and the meek will he teach his way.

*P*salms 25:9

Hear me, O Lord; for thy lovingkindness is good:
turn unto me according to the multitude of thy tender mercies.

*P*salms 69:16

I will go before thee,
and make the crooked places straight.

Isaiah 45:2

Give us day by day our daily bread.

Luke 11:3

Let your light so shine before men,
that they may see your good works,
and glorify your Father which is in heaven.

*M*atthew 5:16

He shall deliver the island of the innocent:
and it is delivered by the pureness of thine hands.

Job 22:30

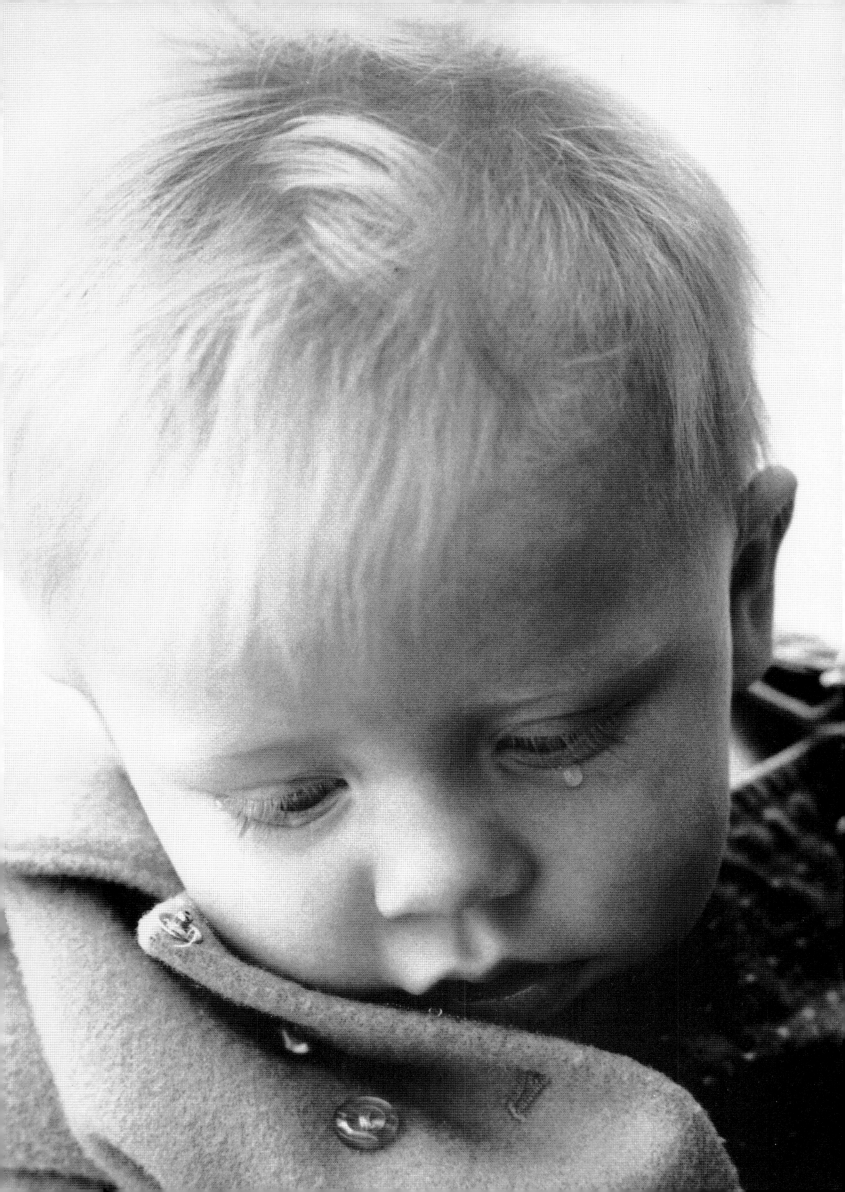

When thou liest down, thou shalt not be afraid:
yea, thou shalt lie down, and thy sleep shall be sweet.

Proverbs 3:24

What is man, that thou art mindful of him?
and the son of man, that thou visitest him?
Thou madest him to have dominion
over the works of thy hands.

Psalms 8:4,6

Hold thou me up, and I shall be safe.

*P*salms 119:117

The fruit of the Spirit is love, joy, peace, longsuffering, gentleness, goodness, faith, meekness, temperance: against such there is no law.

Galatians 5:22, 23

With joy shall ye draw water out
of the wells of salvation.

Isaiah 12:3

The Lord is good to all:
and his tender mercies are over all his works.

Psalms 145:9

Be ye glad and rejoice for ever
in that which I create: for, behold,
I create Jerusalem a rejoicing,
and her people a joy.

Isaiah 65:18

God hath made me to laugh,
so that all that hear will laugh with me.

Genesis 21:6

Not that we are sufficient of ourselves
to think any thing as of ourselves;
but our sufficiency is of God.

II Corinthians 3:5

The Lord is my shepherd; I shall not want.

$\mathcal{P}$salms 23:1

My people shall dwell in a peaceable habitation,
and in sure dwellings, and in quiet resting places.

*I*saiah 32:18

Unto thee, O Lord, do I lift up my soul.
O my God, I trust in thee.

*P*salms 25:1, 2

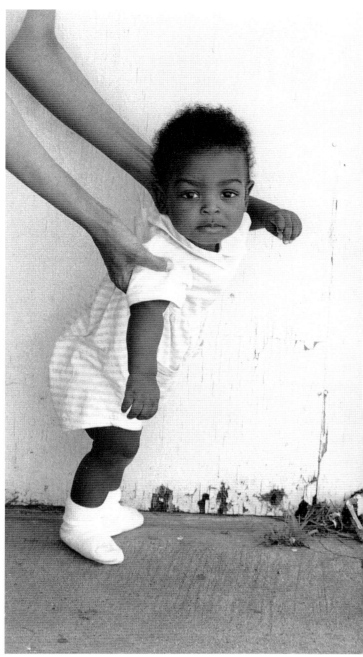

Ye shall go out with joy, and be led forth with peace:
the mountains and the hills shall break forth before you into singing,
and all the trees of the field shall clap their hands.

Isaiah 55:12